THE
TRAILBLAZER GUIDE
to
CROSSES & STONES
on the
NORTH YORK MOORS

Written
&
Compiled

by

J.Brian Beadle

First published in Great Britain in 2003 by Trailblazer Publishing (Scarborough)
www.trailblazerbooks.co.uk

ISBN   1 899004 47 5

ISBN   1 899004 47 5
Trailblazer Publishing (Scarborough)
Stoneways
South End
Burniston
Scarborough. YO13 0HP

Sketches on the cover by the author

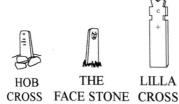

HOB   THE   LILLA
CROSS   FACE STONE   CROSS

CONTENTS

THE NORTH YORK MOORS

The North York Moors are one of the wildest places in Yorkshire. They were formed thousands of years ago when ice melted and formed massive lakes. The water eventually burst out spilling millions of gallons across the moors cutting out deep gorges into the earth. One huge lake, Lake Eskdale, was eleven miles long and over 400 feet deep. As its waters tore through the moors to empty into Lake Pickering it gouged out Newtondale. As the climate became warmer a lush green earth evolved which provided habitation for man.

The moors were probably first inhabited by civilized man called the long headed people. They came from Western Europe and made tools and pottery and had domesticated animals. They buried their dead in long barrows which were communal burial places and the bones were sometimes burned. They lived here about four thousand years ago and it was around this time that the beaker people arrived from Germany and Holland. In contrast to the long headed people the beaker people were round headed. They made fine, coloured pottery and

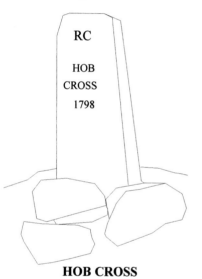

HOB CROSS

were famous for their drinking vessels. The moors have been inhabited throughout centuries, evidence of different civilizations being found in their burial mounds. They left us many memorials to find as we walk across this vast bleak moorland. Tumuli, barrows and mounds abound together with earthworks and curious rocks and stones. The Romans left us their road near Goathland, their training camps near Pickering and the remains of signal stations, but most of them have now fallen into the sea due to coastal erosion.

Crosses appeared to mark the way for travellers, some as a commemoration to brave souls who perished in the fog and snow, some have religious significance and others are simple boundary markers

THE FACE STONE

with the landowners initials inscribed on them. Many crosses are not in the shape of a cross but exist as an erect stone with or without a base. Villages and monasteries sprang up, the crosses guiding travellers around the moors - the crosses and marker stones making useful waymarks. For these moorland tracks were equivalent to the motorways of today. As man became more adventurous he used the tracks to carry goods across the moors on ponies and mules. Some tracks were paved and bore the name of rode, (road) causeways or pannier trods. Many followed the ridges and were called ridgeways to avoid boggy land. The most famous and original medieval ridgeway today is perhaps across Rudland Rigg. The track surface is today identical to its medieval ancestry.

With all this activity and the provision of many guide posts after 1711, leaves us with an abundance of history to explore. This Crucial Guide will, I hope, point you in the right direction to find crosses, ancient stones and old roads on the North York Moors. Happy hunting!

CROSSES OF THE
NORTH YORK MOORS

To make it easier for you to find the crosses and their sites I have listed their grid positions which must be used in relation to an Ordnance Survey map. The best maps of the North York Moors are the large scale Ordnance Survey Outdoor Leisure series numbers 27 Eastern Area and 26 Western Area. There is also a location map in this book to give you an idea of which area they are in.

NAME	GRID REF	
Ainhowe	724938	Original in crypt of Lastingham church
Ann's	878002	Fylingdales Moor
Baysdale	616059	Nr. Baysdale Abbey
Black Hill	742046	Glaisdale Rigg
Botton	697020	Danby High Moor

Cockan	631992	Rudland Rigg - Inscribed waymark
Cooper	515830	Roadside near Sutton Bank car park only the base is left
Donna	545034	Near to Cold Moor - ancient cross dated to 1642 - only the base is left
Esklets	658005	Farndale Moor - no base and laid on ground
Face Stone	597015	Urra Moor - boundary stone with face
Fat Betty	682020	Rosedale Head - chunky white stone with wheel on top, sometimes known as White Cross
Friar's	488899	Marks track from Rievaulx to Helmsley
Hawsker	923076	Hawsker village shaft is 10th cent. has Norse engraving
High	734885	Outskirts of Appleton le Moors village, could have been a marker to the Saxon Monastery at Lastingham
Hob	646134	Guisborough Moor - A superb bound -ary marker engraved with date and initials
Jenny Bradley	612023	Rudland Rigg - small stone on base, overwhelmed by Feversham estate boundary stone
Job	686110	Danby Low Moor - said to be the place of Hobgoblins. Waymarker of paved way to Guisborough
Job	627025	Near to Rudland Rigg - stones laid flat
John	900027	Shooting House Rigg - remains of base fitted with boundary stone
John o'man	615076	Between Baysdale & Kildale at roadside
Lady	815083	Side of A171
Lilla	889987	On Lilla Rigg - superb cross erected to

		the memory of the nobleman Saxon Lilla for saving his king's life by sacrificing his own
Low	734883	On outskirts of Appleton le Moor, could once have been used as the village stocks
Malo	868949	Super Cross at bottom of Whinny Nab near Saltersgate
Mauley	797944	In Cropton Forest near exit onto Egton road Boundary stone named after de Mauleys of Mulgrave Castle
Percy	606118	Guisborough Moor - rough base left
Postgate	918044	Adjacent to A171 near junction with B1416 - old post road from Pickering to Whitby
Ralph,Old	675020	Westerdale Moor near Rosedale and Westerdale junction. Many tales surround Ralph's Cross. Some say a man called Ralph perished in a blizzard here. Others tell the tale of Ralph guiding two nuns in a fog to their meeting place
Ralph, Young	677022	Near Old Ralph
Redman	732936	Spaunton Moor - large base, no shaft. Used as a bird feeder!
Robinson's	486956	Near Osmotherley on roadside. Boundary marker
Roppa North	587930	Helmsley Moor
Roppa South	588924	Helmsley Moor
Rosedale	736967	Top of Haygate Bank
Scawton	549836	Scawton village - not much left
Scale	674089	Between Commondale and Castleton
Siss	704105	Danby Low Moor

Steeple	495902	Hambleton Drove Road Boundary Stone 1770
Stump	745095	Lealholm Moor - marker at Stoxla Rd and Waupley track
Stump	607983	Bransdale Moor - waymark cross
Swarth Howe	841086	Near Briggswath - boundary stone
Victoria	728901	Overlooking Lastingham and the moors, erected in 1897 for Queen Victoria's Diamond Jubilee
White	681108	Danby Low Moor
White	682020	See Fat Betty
York	878015	Sneaton High Moor on Whinstone Ridge way mark cross

THE MORE IMPORTANT CROSSES

These crosses are generally in good condition, have a special feature or mark an important route across the moors. I will describe them in more detail.

Lilla Cross

Perhaps the best and earliest example of a moor land cross existing onthe North York Moors. It is hewn from a single piece of stone and is engraved with the Comley estate mark. It is said to be the burial place of the red haired Lilla but excavations found jewellery from a couple of centuries after the death of Lilla. Lilla was a Saxon nobleman who died saving his king's life by throwing himself between the king and his assailant. A sword was thrust into Lilla's body, he fell to the ground his red hair mingling with his spent blood. The Saxons are said to have erected this cross for Lilla to commemorate his supposed burial place high upon the

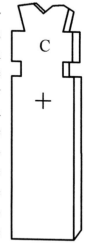

moors which is one of the most beautiful places to be. From this high vantage point the all round views are spectacular. I'm sure Lilla would have approved.

Mauley Cross

Mauley Cross stands on the edge of Cropton Forest sheltered by trees. Different to the day it was erected when it would have looked across open land from its high vantage point. It is a large cross hewn from a single piece of stone with curves for corners. It marked the boundary of the lands of the De Mauley family of Mulgrave Castle near Whitby. It is a well preserved example of a period cross.

Malo Cross

Malo Cross is another fine example of a 17th century moorland cross. It is marked with the letters R, E and K. They stand for Richard Egerton, Knight. He is said to have placed the cross in this position to try to extend his lands into the royal hunting forest of Pickering. Its uncanny position is also on a branch of the Pannierman's Way from Lilla Cross and could have been used as a guide for weary travellers. Its head is unusual having rounded arms and seems to be younger than the lower shaft. There is no base. Probably the reason why it is now leaning over. The cross disappeared in the 19th century and was found in a garden in Pickering! Thankfully now re-erected for us all to enjoy.

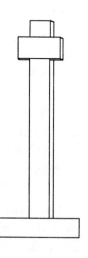

Aine Howe Cross

The wilds of Spaunton Moor haven't changed much since the search for iron ore ended in the early 1900's. Only the scars are left as evidence of the area's industrial heritage of its mining days. At the top of Rosedale Bank Top there are some old kilns still standing and evidence of railway tracks. It is at bank Top that you set off across the moor again to visit Ana Cross, now restored to its full glory dominating the skyline once more. The original Ana Cross, or Ain Howe Cross to give it its correct name, is in the church at Lastingham. Ana Cross is the tallest on the moors and has been a landmark for hundreds of years guiding lost souls over these bleak moors.

Hob Cross

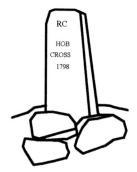

Hob cross stands in the wilderness between Guisborough Moor and Stanghowe Moor. It is an impressive boundary stone. Standing at the cross you will see many boundary stones reaching across the moor and on the horizon, one of which is the stone known as Hob on the Hill. Hob Cross is inscribed with the initials of Robert Chaloner who owned lands around these parts. Also its name and the date 1798.

Fat Betty

Situated at the head of the Rosedale valley Fat Betty, or White Cross is an unusal piece of stone. It has a large chunky white stone for its base, hence the name fat, and a wheel cross on top. It is a boundary stone and is painted white to, as an old moors man once said, to show the grouse which side of the boundary they belonged! The cross is sometimes known as White Cross for obvious reasons. It is usally given the Fat Betty name to avoid confusion with the other White Cross near Castleton.

Old Ralph's Cross

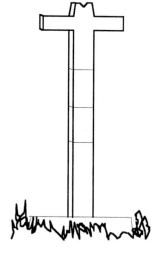

Westerdale Moor near the Rosedale and Westerdale junction. Many tales surround Ralph's Cross. Some say a man called Ralph perished in a blizzard here. But there is a goodly tale of a guide called 'Ord Ralph Rosdil' who guided the prioresses of Baysdale Abbey and Rosedale Abbey during a boundary dispute. It is said that they were lost in a fog and Ralph found one Prioress, Sister Margery, sitting on the Margery Bradley Stone. He found the other Prioress, Sister Betty, sitting on the Fat Betty Cross. He guided them safely to the site of Old Ralphs Cross for their meeting.

TUMULI

Our ancient ancestors left us with their burialgrounds high on the North York Moors. Some large graves and some small. They are called Howes, Barrows and Cairns. They were built by Saxons and Danes when they buried their more important citizens. Chiefs, tribal leaders and warriors are buried in these graves and there are two types to be found.

The single Tumuli or grave would have a large stone slab over the body and there would be many of the persons possessions buried with them. The second type would be found not with a skeleton but urns. Each urn having the burnt and charred bones of different people. There are hundreds of these Tumuli dotted around the moors I have listed the location of many of them complete with grid references to help you find them.

LEGEND

RB= Round Barrow.   HW=Howe.
SC=Stone Circle.   LB= Long Barrow.

GRID REF	DESCRIPTION	
010876	Seamer Beacon	
011872	" "	Group of RB
522013	Busby Moor	RB
560823	Scawton Moor	RB
565820	" "	RB
583820	Sproxton Moor	RB
584929	Helmsley Moor	RB
587930 & 591923	Bilsdale	Three RB
625132	Guisborough, Near Penrod Hill	HW
625137	" " "	HW
626136	" " "	HW
666125	High Moor - Black Howes	HW
667004	Farndale Moor - South Flat Howe	RB
673013	Farndale Moor - Flat Howe	RB

11

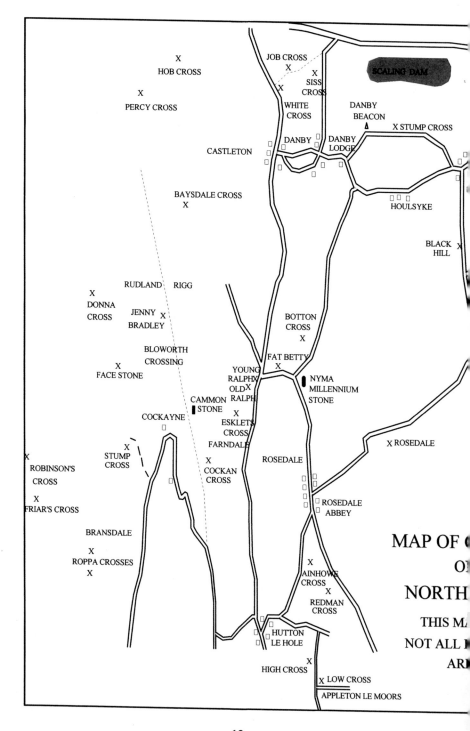

X
HOB CROSS

JOB CROSS
X
X
SISS
CROSS
X

SCALING DAM

X
PERCY CROSS

WHITE
CROSS

DANBY
BEACON

X STUMP CROSS

CASTLETON

DANBY

DANBY
LODGE

BAYSDALE CROSS
X

HOULSYKE

BLACK
HILL
X

RUDLAND RIGG

X
DONNA
CROSS

JENNY X
BRADLEY

BOTTON
CROSS
X

BLOWORTH
CROSSING

X
FACE STONE

FAT BETTY
X

YOUNG
RALPH X
OLD X
RALPH

NYMA
MILLENNIUM
STONE

CAMMON
STONE

COCKAYNE

X
ESKLETS
CROSS

FARNDALE

ROSEDALE

X
STUMP
CROSS

X
COCKAN
CROSS

X ROSEDALE

X
ROBINSON'S
CROSS

ROSEDALE
ABBEY

X
FRIAR'S CROSS

BRANSDALE
X
ROPPA CROSSES
X

X
AINHOWE
CROSS
X
REDMAN
CROSS

MAP OF (
O
NORTH

THIS M
NOT ALL
AR

HUTTON
LE HOLE

X
HIGH CROSS

X LOW CROSS
APPLETON LE MOORS

12

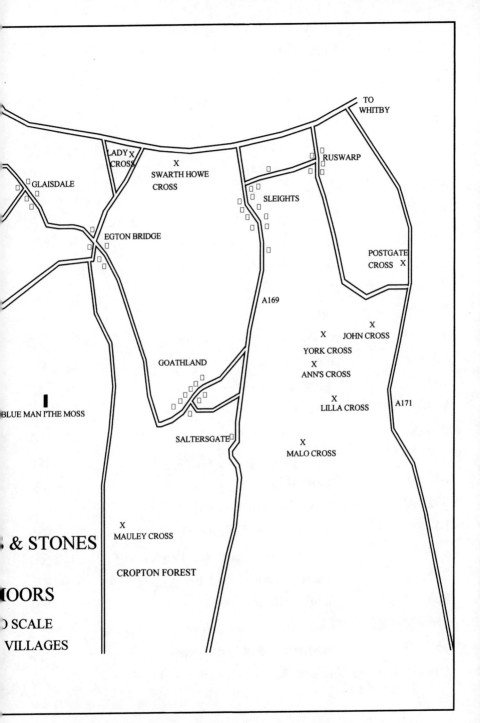

TO
WHITBY

LADY X
CROSS

SWARTH HOWE
CROSS
X

GLAISDALE

RUSWARP

SLEIGHTS

EGTON BRIDGE

POSTGATE
CROSS X

A169

JOHN CROSS
X
X

YORK CROSS
X

GOATHLAND

ANN'S CROSS
X

BLUE MAN I'THE MOSS

LILLA CROSS
X

A171

SALTERSGATE

MALO CROSS
X

& STONES

MAULEY CROSS
X

CROPTON FOREST

OORS

SCALE

VILLAGES

679998	Blakey Moor - Blakey Howe	RB
680994	Blakey Moor - Little Blakey Howe	RB
682105	Danby Low Moor - Three Howes	HW
687096	Danby Low Moor - Pike Howe	HW
704118	Gerrick Moor - Herd Howe	HW
725861	Off Spaunton Moor	Two RB
730102	Danby Low Moor - Nean Howe	HW
735093	Danby Beacon	Two RB
745095	Lealholme Moor - Brown Rigg Howe	RB
755094	Lealholme Rigg - Rawland Howe	HW
762138	Roxby Low Moor - Stang Howe	HW
776144	Borrowby Moor	LB
784116	Ugthorpe - Loose Howe	HW
795135	Ellerby Moor - Stump Howe	HW
820880	Blansby Park	Four RB
823077	Egton Low Moor	Two RB
829878	Blansby Park	RB
829889	Levisham - Ness Head	RB
833138	Potato Hill - Barnby Howe	HW
837079	Egton Moor	Two RB
842090	Hutton Mulgrave Wood	RB
848942	Lockton - near Gallows Dike	Three RB
854035	Sleights Moor - Breckon Howe	RB
856046	Sleights Moor - Flat Howes	Two RB
857037	Sleights Moor	RB
859999	Goathland - Widow Howe	HW
868019	Goathland - Robbed Howe	HW
869036	Sleights Moor - Greenland's Howe	RB

873935	Blakey Topping	SC
874009	Widow Howe Moor - Foster Howe	RB
879016	York Cross	RB
887992	Fylingdales Moor - Louven Howe	RB
889988	Lilla Rigg - Lilla Howe	HW
911036	Low Moor - Thorn Key Howes	HW
924045	Latter Gate Hills	RB's
942880	Wykeham Forest	SC + RB's
942998	Jugger Howe Moor - Jugger Howe	RB
944002	Jugger Howe Moor - Jugger Howes	RB's
946005	Stony Marl Moor	SC
915033	Fylingdales Moor - Thorn Key Howes	SC+RB's
950891	Wykeham Forest	RB
951010	Howdale Moor	Group of RB
953893	Mount Misery	RB
955022	Brow Moor - Robin Hood's Butts	RB's
956877	Wykeham Forest	RB
956891	Wykeham Forest	SC + RB's
958873	Hutton Buscel	RB
962007	Stony Marl Moor - Stony Marl Howes	RB
962890	Wykeham Forest	Three RB
963991	Harwood Dale - Penny Howes	RB
967000	Harwood Dale	RB
970995	Harwood Dale	RB
972991	Harwood Dale	RB
973012	Beacon Howes	RB's
976998	Staintondale Moor	RB's
978010	Ravenscar	RB
978985	Staintondale	RB

979971	Harwood Dale - Standing Stone Rigg	RB's
981969	Harwood Dale - Standing Stone Rigg	SC
983969	Harwood Dale Forest - Standing Stones Rigg	SC
983991	Staintondale	RB
987012	Ravenscar	RB
995965	Cloughton Moor	RB
997878	Irton Moor	RB

LINEAR EARTHWORKS

007883	Rowbrow Wood - Earthwork
778035	Egton Grange - Settlement & Dike
847942	Saltergate Hill - Gallows Dike
858944	Hazelhead Moor - Double Dike
882852	Dalby Forest - Glendale Dike
894852	Scamridge - Scamridge Dikes
904022	Shooting House Rigg - Earthwork
915867	Cockmoor Hall - Six Dikes
923047	Near A171 - Earthwork
958875	Wykeham Forest - Moor Dike
970005	Stony Marl Moor - Green Dike
975928	Silpho - Thieves Dikes

CASTLES

There were many castles or fortified houses built, very few on the high moors though and many are on the fringes of the moors.
I submit a simple list of these castles, many are only sites, but may be of interest to you. The name is followed by a grid reference where the exact site is known.

Ayton	985853	Near village
Brompton	945822	Was on castle hill
Castleton	692083	Motte only
Danby	717073	14 century. part of castle still stands and is used
Cropton	755894	Site only
Helmsley	610835	Built in 12th century. Sieged once in 1644 in its uneventful history. Good remains to be seen.
Kilton	703178	Nr. Skelton, haunted by Lucia de Thweng
Malton	793718	Site of important Roman Fort
Mulgrave 1	832118	Originally called Fosse Castle only the motte remains. Was home of Saxon Duke Wada or Wade
Mulgrave 2	840117	Norman. Ivy - clad remains in Mulgrave Woods. Currently under restoration. Beautiful setting on ridge between two valleys although the trees now deny us the view the Normans would have had
Mulgrave 3	845126	The home of the Marquis of Normanby on opposite ridge to Mulgrave 2
Pickering	799845	Well preserved motte & bailey. Built 14th century but original timber castle would have been built much earlier. Used as hunting lodge when Pickering Forest existed
Scarborough	050892	On magnificent headland, built 12th century and was visited by kings of the realm. Lots to see including good grounds and superb views. Saw military action and was sieged. Shelled by German navy in 1914. It is said to be

haunted by Piers Gaveston who was
once the custodian and was beheaded.
The headless Piers is said to walk the
walls at dusk.

Wilton   863827   Built 1807, no remains

ABBEYS

Abbeys were built in profusion all over Yorkshire. Nestling in the fertile valleys many inhabitants found a good life whilst following their faith. I have listed all I know around the area. Most are now just sites but it is interesting to know where these people lived. A map reference of the known location follows the name.

NR = no remains

Baysdale   621067   Cistercian nuns - house
                      named Baysdale Abbey on site - NR

Byland   550789   Cistercian, built 1177
                      very good ruin to visit. Lots to see including
                      old pavement

Goathland   Benedictine - off A169, eight miles SW of Whitby - NR

Grosmont   Benedictine - off A169 two miles nearer Whitby than
                      Goathland Abbey - NR

Guisborough Priory 618161 Augustinian impressive grounds and
                      ruins in Guisborough town built in 1199. It
                      is said a hidden chest of gold is guarded by a
                      Raven that is the reincarnation of 'Old Nick'
                      himself!

Hackness   970906   Benedictine church now built over site - NR

Hutton   Cistercian nuns, built 1162 near Guisborough - NR

Keldhome   Cistercian nuns - SE of Kirkbymoorside, built 1130 - NR

Kildale Friary   Crutched friars built 1312 - NR

Lastingham 730904   Benedictine, church built on site - built 654 -
                      good haunted crypt. Lots of history here about
                      early christianity - NR

Rievaulx	576850	Cistercian - built 1131, absolutely superb ruin cared for by English Heritage
Rosedale	724959	Cistercian nuns - built 1190, one pillar remains in village near school
Scalby Friary		Franciscan friars - NR
Scawton	549836	Cistercian five miles west of Helmsley built 1146 - NR
Scarborough Friary		Franciscan built 1239 - Dominican built 1252, Carmelite built 1319 - NR
Stocking		Cistercian, close to Scawton - built 1147 - NR
Whitby	903113	Benedictine - original abbey built 657 but was rebuilt many times. Superb ruin now cared for by English Heritage
Wykeham		Cistercian nuns - built 1153. Now a private estate and house

OTHER INTERESTING FEATURES

Caves

King Alfred's	898833	Ebberston built as monument in 1793 to mark battle in 705 between Oswy, king of Northumbria and his son Alfred who is said to have shelterd in a cave nearby with fatal wounds
Kirkdale	678856	In side of cliff near ford off A170 between Helmsley and Kirkbymoorside. Prehistoric remains have been found there

Hermitages

Eskdaleside	On south bank of River Esk near railway remains of hermitage of the Monk of Whitby
Goathland	One mile from Goathland chapel at Abbots House farm is the site of a hermitage

May Beck	Built as folly out of solid rock dated 1790, a rock seat is carved on top of the cave
Mulgrave Woods	At eastern end, it juts from ridge between two becks - now used as summerhouse
Solomon's Temple	Building by hermit Matt Walker. Not completed and is a ruin. It is situated alongside the Osmotherley road near the Chequers tea rooms, once a drovers drinking place called the Cheq uers Inn

Miscellaneous

One mile NE of Kilburn at Hood Monastery there are 2 stone coffins one of which is built into the side of a barn

John Bond's Sheephouse	898014	Walled enclosure in trees on Fylingdales Moor
Lady Mary Ross's Seat	594055	On the route of one of Lady Mary's favourite walks

WATER MILLS

OLD

Arden	521907
Bransdale	621979
Caydale	545867
Lastingham	728905

19th CENTURY

Bilsdale	571953
Danby	707083
Farndale	668970
Kilton	717190
Levisham	835902
Raisdale	538005
Rosedale	724957
Tocketts	628183

STANDING STONES OF INTEREST

Blue Man I'the Moss 765992 On Wheeldale Howe - a huge stone marking the junction of three boundaries

Cammon Stone 626000 On Rudland Rigg. The west side is inscribed *Hallelujah* in Arabic and is said to be the work off an eccentric clergyman of the last century

Jenny Bradley 612023 Rudland Rigg - small stone on base, overwhelmed by Feversham estate boundary stone

Hand Stone 597015 On Urra Moor - could be marking Celtic graves

Hanging Stone 585929 On Roppa Moor on top of tumulus now fallen over at angle

Margery Bradley Stone 675013 On the side of the Castleton to Hutton le Hole road is a large slab to which boundaries of Feversham Estates were drawn. She was called Breadless in earlier years. See also Ralph's Cross

Millennium 697013 North York Moors Association stone at side of road

Old Wife's Neck 902021 On Shooting Howe Rigg. Said to be Bell the giant Wade's wife turned to stone

Roadmen's 676012 Marks the boundary of a section of roadmen's working area

Temple Beele 756103 Five large slabs erected in form of cross south of Scaling Dam on Danby Estate.

Wade's 830130/830146 These two stones were named after the legendary giant Wade who lived at Lythe. Or was it the Saxon Duke Wada who was responsible for this legend, or were they the same person?

| Wainstones | 559036 | On Cold Moor. They are natural rocks with an Alpine like facade in miniature. There is a steeple and a sphinx. The rocks are climbed by the local climbing club. Although they are on the very edge of the North York Moors they are impressive rocks and as a bonus the view from this point is superb. |

WINDMILLS

Kirkbymoorside	696683
Ravenscar	976006
Ugthorpe	789116

OLD ROADS

Unlike today's transport medieval man had either to walk or travel by horse. He used wide earth roads along ridges called ridgeways for his carts They were either dusty, muddy or snowbound and full of potholes. Guide stones weren't in place before 1711 and there were no maps. Roads were not made they were created, someone wanted to go somewhere so they made tracks and others followed! Many of these old roads and ridgeways are almost in original condition. We can walk these old roads and imagine what life must have been like for the Drovers and Carters.

Thurkilsti

This important road Thurkil's Hill Road (Thurkilsti) went from Welburn, although it could have started at York but I have no evidence of this. It traversed Bransdale Ridge to end up at Battersby. Not much left of the old road now.

Magna Via

Starting from helmsley the road soon took to the ridges over Helmsley Moors and onto Bilsdale. It eventually reached Stump Cross where it joined Thurkilsti.

Waingate and Rudland Rigg

This road was an alternative to the Magna via and Thurkilsti roads. It starts as Waingate from Kirkbymoorside market place and past the old castle along to Gilamoor. Straight ahead now still climbing onto Rudland Rigg. The Rigg is still an earth road across this high ridge with Bransdale on one side and Farndale on the other it is an extremely scenic road. It continues along past Bloworth crossing and the old ironstone railway track to end at Ingleby Greenhow.

Hambleton Street

This is the majestic King's Way, the Regalis Via and is the best pre served drove road in the area. It is a true ridgeway traversing the heights of Black Hambleton on its way to the great fairs and markets of medieval times. It was used by drovers who drove cattle from the north to the markets in the south. There were inns along the Hambleton Street alas only ruins remain apart from Chequers which is now tea rooms near Osmotherley but still has an old sign above the door which says 'Free ale for nothing, tomorrow'. Of course, tomorrow never comes!

If you wish to walk the old road it runsfrom Dialstone Farm (GR 519842) near Sutton Bank on a tarmac road joining the off road track at Sneck Yate Bank (GR 510877) passing over the Hambleton Hills to Black Hambleton and the road near Osmotherley (GR480956).

Wade's Causeway

Legend says that Wade's Causeway was built by the giant Wade for his giant wife Bell to make her way across the moors to milk her cow. But history tells us that it was built by the Romans to march their Legions across the moors quickly from Malton to the signal stations on the coast. It is the best preserved Roman road in the country and gives us some idea of what the construction of a Roman road was like. The remains seen today are only the foundations. You can see a short stretch of the road from the Stape to Egton road at GR 803972 where there is a gate and a sign pointing you in the right direction allowing you to walk by the side of the road across Wheeldale Moor towards Goathland.

TRAILBLAZER BOOKS

CYCLING BOOKS
Mountain Biking around the Yorkshire Dales
Mountain Biking the Easy Way
Mountain Biking in North Yorkshire
Mountain Biking on the Yorkshire Wolds
Mountain Biking for Pleasure
Mountain Biking in the Lake District
Mountain Biking around Ryedale, Wydale & the North York Moors
Exploring Ryedale, Moor & Wold by Bicycle
Beadle's Bash - 100 mile challenge route for Mountain Bikers

WALKING BOOKS
Walking into History on the Dinosaur Coast
Walking in Heartbeat Country
Walking in Captain Cook's Footsteps
Walking the Ridges & Riggs of the North York Moors
Short Walks around the Yorkshire Coast
Walking on the Yorkshire Coast
Walking to Abbeys, Castles & Churches
Walking around the North York Moors
Walking around Scarborough, Whitby & Filey
Walking to Crosses on the North York Moors
Walks from the Harbour
Walking in Dalby, the Great Yorkshire Forest
Ten Scenic Walks around Rosedale, Farndale & Hutton le Hole
Twelve Scenic Walks from the North Yorkshire Moors Railway
Twelve Scenic Walks around the Yorkshire Dales
Twelve Scenic Walks around Ryedale, Pickering & Helmsley

DOING IT YOURSELF SERIES
Make & Publish Your Own Books

THE EXPLORER SERIES
Exploring Ryedale, Moor & Wold by Bicycle

YORKSHIRE BOOKS
Curious Goings on in Yorkshire
The Trailblazer Guide to Crosses & Stones on the North York Moors

**For more information please visit our web site:
www.trailblazerbooks.co.uk**